MACMILLAN READERS

ELEMENTARY LEVE

JOHNS

The Mark ʋɾɾo ™

Retold by Anne Collins

A 6 2
A 6 5 6 = Mooefaz Draw out

≋ MACMILLAN

Founding Editor: John Milne

The Macmillan Readers provide a choice of enjoyable reading materials for learners of English. The series is published at six levels – Starter, Beginner, Elementary, Pre-intermediate, Intermediate and Upper.

Level control
Information, structure and vocabulary are controlled to suit the students' ability at each level.

The number of words at each level: NZ ONE 3

Starter	about 300 basic words
Beginner	about 600 basic words
Elementary	about 1100 basic words
Pre-intermediate	about 1400 basic words
Intermediate	about 1600 basic words
Upper	about 2200 basic words

Vocabulary
Some difficult words and phrases in this book are important for understanding the story. Some of these words are explained in the story and some are shown in the pictures. From Pre-intermediate level upwards, words are marked with a number like this: ...[3]. These words are explained in the Glossary at the end of the book.

Contents

A Note About This Story

Johnston McCulley was born in Ottawa, Illinois, in the U.S.A., on February 2nd, 1883. He died in California, on November 23rd, 1958. He wrote hundred of stories— detective stories, crime stories, mysteries, westerns. McCulley wrote 64 stories about the masked hero, Zorro. The first story was called *The Curse of Capistrano* and it was published in a magazine in 1919. In 1920, the movie actor Douglas Fairbanks read the story. He liked it very much. He made a movie—*The Mark of Zorro*—from the story. It was extremely successful. The story was published again in 1924. This time, it was called *The Mark of Zorro*. Since 1920, many movies, TV shows and cartoons have been made about Zorro. Two of the most popular were made in 1940 and 1998.

The Mark of Zorro takes place in California in about 1822. It is not a true story. At that time, California was owned by Spain. It was not part of the U.S.A. until 1850. The Governor of California lived in Mexico City. At this time, Los Angeles was a small town. A governor in San Francisco looked after it.

a sword

a scabbard

a whip

a pistol

a carriage

The People in This Story

Sergeant Gonzales

Don Diego Vega

Don Carlos
Pulido

Doña Catalina
Pulido

Señorita Lolita
Pulido

Captain Ramón

Don Alejandro
Vega

Fray Felipe

Zorro

The Governor of
California

1

A Stormy Night

One dark night in February, a group of soldiers were sitting in a small inn. The inn was on one side of Los Angeles town square. Outside, the weather was wild and stormy. Rain was crashing on the roof and the wind was making a terrible noise. But inside, it was bright and comfortable. The soldiers sat in front of a warm fire, drinking wine and playing cards.

"Bring more wine, landlord!" shouted a big man with a moustache, to the owner of the inn. The man with the moustache was the soldiers' leader, Sergeant Gonzales.

"Yes, *señor!*" said the fat landlord. He hurried to fill Gonzales's cup with wine. He was afraid of the big sergeant. Sergeant Gonzales was a strong man and he became angry very easily. He often fought with other soldiers.

"Talking is better than fighting," thought the landlord. "What can I say that will interest Gonzales?"

"People in the town are talking about Señor Zorro," he said quickly. "He has been seen in Los Angeles again."

Gonzales threw his cup of wine onto the floor.

"Señor Zorro!" he cried out in a terrible voice. "Must I always hear that name? I hate it! This man, Zorro, is very clever. Nobody knows who he is. Nobody has seen his face. He wears a black mask with two holes for his eyes. He cuts the faces of his enemies with his sword. He marks them with a shape like the letter Z. People call it the Mark of Zorro."

"But Zorro has never visited us here, Sergeant," said the landlord nervously.

"No," said Gonzales. "And why not? Because *I'm* here and he's afraid of me. I'm the best soldier in the Governor of California's army!"

"Has Señor Zorro ever killed anybody?" asked the landlord.

"No—not yet," replied Gonzales slowly. "He tells people, 'I'm not a real thief. I only punish the enemies of the poor and the weak.' But Zorro's days will soon be over," Gonzales went on. "The governor has offered a reward for him. He'll pay a lot of money to the man who kills Zorro."

"I don't want Zorro to come here," said the landlord.

"Let him come!" shouted Gonzales. "I'm waiting for him. I'll kill him and I'll get the reward. I'll—"

Suddenly the door opened, and a man walked into the inn.

Everybody stared at him in surprise. Gonzales pulled his sword from its scabbard. He was ready to fight. But the man was not Zorro—it was Don Diego Vega.

The Vega family was one of the richest families in southern California. They had lived there for many years. They owned a large amount of land, and a huge number of cattle and horses. Don Diego—the only son of the noble family—was twenty-four years old and he was very handsome. He owned a beautiful *hacienda*—a large country house—and also a fine house in Los Angeles. This town house was opposite the inn.

Don Diego was different from most of the other young men in the town. He did not enjoy loud talk or fighting. He was not interested in winning the love of women. He liked music, poetry and quiet conversation.

Don Diego and Sergeant Gonzales were very different kinds of men, but they were friends. Don Diego often

7

bought wine for Gonzales, and he liked to listen to the sergeant's conversation.

Sergeant Gonzales put his sword back into its scabbard.

"I'm sorry, my friend," he said to Don Diego. "I didn't want to frighten you. I couldn't see your face in the darkness. We were just talking about that thief, Zorro."

"Not Zorro again!" said Diego in a tired voice. He looked bored. "I don't like stories about blood and violence. You know that! I really don't want to hear about Zorro."

"But the governor has offered a very good reward for him," Gonzales answered. "And I'm going to get it. I'm going to catch Zorro. I'll tell you all about it when I get the reward. I'll tell you how I caught him, how I killed him—"

"Gonzales, please don't talk about killing," said Don Diego. "I've heard enough!"

He called to the landlord. "Give Sergeant Gonzales more wine," he said. "Then perhaps he'll stop talking."

The landlord hurried to bring wine for the two men. Don Diego drank his wine slowly, but Gonzales drank very quickly. After half an hour, Don Diego stood up.

"I have to go home now," he said.

"But the weather is very bad," said Gonzales. "My soldiers will go with you. They'll take you home safely."

"No, no," replied Don Diego. "Let them stay here by the fire. I don't need soldiers. Give your men some more wine. I will pay for it later. Good night."

"Good night, señor," everybody said.

When Don Diego had gone, Gonzales spoke to his soldiers.

"That young man is very unusual," he said. "He isn't interested in fighting. He isn't interested in winning the

The landlord hurried to bring wine for the two men.

love of women. But he is my good friend. He's a fine young man!"

All the soldiers agreed with Gonzales. Don Diego was going to pay for their wine, so they were very happy. The fat landlord was happy too.

Sergeant Gonzales stood up and he pulled out his sword again. He waved it in the air.

"Don Diego doesn't like fighting," he shouted, "but I do. Why doesn't Zorro come now? I'm ready for him!"

At that moment, the door opened again and a stranger entered the room!

2

The Man in the Mask

The stranger stood in the dark shadows by the door. His large *sombrero* was pulled down over his eyes. He wore a long dark cloak around his body.

The landlord hurried towards him. Then the stranger stepped forward into the light. Now everybody could see him clearly. The landlord stopped and cried out in fear. Gonzales's eyes were wide with surprise. The stranger was wearing a black mask. There were two holes in the mask. Through these holes, his bright eyes were watching everything.

"I'm Señor Zorro," replied the man. "And I'm here to speak to *you*." He pointed at Gonzales.

"What do you mean?" asked Gonzales.

"I know what kind of man you are, Sergeant Gonzales," replied Zorro. "Four days ago you stopped a man on the road and beat him cruelly. The man was poor and weak. He hadn't done anything wrong. I'm a friend of that poor man. I've come to punish you!"

Zorro was telling the truth. Gonzales *had* beaten a man on the road. The sergeant remembered that. But then he remembered the governor's reward too, and he smiled.

"Very well, Señor Zorro," he said. "We will fight."

He pulled out his sword and walked towards Zorro. But Zorro put his hand under his cloak and brought out a pistol. He pointed the gun at Gonzales.

"What's this?" said Gonzales. He began to laugh. "Are you going to shoot me with your pistol? You aren't very brave, Señor Zorro. You're afraid of my sword. It's very easy to kill somebody with a pistol. But a sword-fight is difficult."

"There are many of your men in this room," Zorro replied. "We will fight with swords, but it must be a fair fight." He pointed the pistol at the soldiers and the landlord.

"Get back," he said to them. "Stand by the wall."

The soldiers and the landlord stood against the wall.

"I'm going to fight with my sword in my right hand. But I'll hold the pistol in my left," Zorro told them. "I'll shoot anybody who moves."

Then he turned towards Gonzales. "Now, señor, I'm ready to begin," he said.

Gonzales ran towards Zorro with his sword, but Zorro's sword pushed it away. Again and again, Gonzales tried to attack Zorro. He tried many tricks, but he could never reach Zorro's body with his sword. Zorro's eyes were bright behind the mask. He was smiling.

Gonzales did not fight well. He had drunk too much wine, and he was getting tired.

When Zorro saw this, he moved forward and began to

Then Zorro turned towards Gonzales. "Now, señor, I'm
ready to begin," he said.

attack Gonzales. Slowly, he pushed the sergeant back against the wall. Zorro was not smiling anymore. His eyes were cold and angry behind the mask.

Suddenly, Zorro moved quickly and knocked Gonzales's sword out of his hand. It fell on the floor with a loud noise. Gonzales closed his eyes. He was ready to die.

But at that moment, the door opened again. A large group of men from the town came in. They were looking for food and drink.

Zorro could not fight so many men. He put his sword back into its scabbard and he jumped onto a chair near a window.

"We haven't finished our fight, señor!" he said to Gonzales. "Goodbye, until the next time!"

Then Zorro jumped through the window and disappeared into the night. The soldiers rushed out of the inn. But they could not see anything in the darkness and the rain. Zorro had escaped.

The soldiers went back into the warm room.

"Did you see Zorro?" Gonzales was saying to the men from the town. "That man doesn't fight in a fair way. He will only use a pistol, not a sword. I had to throw my sword to the ground!"

Gonzales was not telling the truth. But nobody disagreed with him.

A minute later, Don Diego hurried back into the inn.

"What's happening here?" he asked. "What's all this noise?"

"Señor Zorro was here," replied Gonzales.

"Was he?" asked Don Diego. "But where is his dead body?"

The landlord and the soldiers smiled. Gonzales's face became red.

"Well—there is no body," he said.

"Have your men taken it away?" asked Don Diego. "Tell me all about the fight. Tell me how you caught him, how you killed him—" Don Diego laughed. "Now you will get your reward, Sergeant!"

Gonzales did not say anything. The soldiers watched him.

"Why are you quiet, my friend?" Don Diego went on. "I don't understand. You did kill Zorro, didn't you?"

"Zorro escaped," said Gonzales at last. "He had a pistol. He got away."

"Well, why didn't you take his pistol from him?" asked Don Diego. "Tell me. I don't understand about fighting." He shouted to the landlord. "Bring more wine for Sergeant Gonzales!"

But Gonzales did not want any more wine. "I have to speak to the *comandante*," he said. "I must tell him about the fight. Good night."

Before Gonzales left the inn, he turned and shouted, "But next time I meet Señor Zorro, I'll kill him!"

Don Diego looked towards the fire and he smiled.

3

Don Diego Wants a Wife

Next morning, the storm was finished. The golden sun shone in a blue sky.

Don Diego Vega was riding his horse along a hot dusty road. He was wearing fine clothes and he was riding very slowly. He was going to make an important visit. He was going to visit the Pulido family.

The Pulidos were an old and noble family. But Don Carlos Pulido had done some things which made the Governor of California angry. Because of this, the governor had taken a lot of land and money from Don Carlos. Now, the Pulidos were a poor family.

Don Carlos was sitting on the veranda of his hacienda. He was sitting in a comfortable chair. The veranda was cool and shady. Don Carlos was very surprised to see Don Diego.

"Nobody visits the Pulidos any more," he said to himself. "What does this young man from the great Vega family want?"

A few moments later, Don Diego came onto the veranda.

"Welcome, Don Diego," Don Carlos said to the young man. "Please sit down. Would you like some cake and wine?"

"Thank you," replied Don Diego in a tired voice. "The weather is so hot and I've ridden a long way."

Don Carlos smiled. The journey from the town to his house was only four miles. It was easy for a young man to ride a powerful horse this distance.

A servant brought some wine. Then Don Diego spoke again.

"Don Carlos, I'm nearly twenty-five years old," he said. "Yesterday, my father talked seriously to me. He wants me to get married. He wants me to have children. The Vega family is an old and noble one. So I must choose a wife from the same kind of family. The Pulido family is a noble family. You have a daughter, Don Carlos."

"Yes," said Don Carlos. "My daughter, Lolita, is eighteen years old now."

"I've seen her several times," said Don Diego. "She's

Don Carlos was very surprised to see Don Diego.

beautiful and clever. Don Carlos, please may I marry her?"

Don Carlos was excited. This was a wonderful thing for the Pulido family. The Vega family were friends of the Governor of California.

"Perhaps Don Diego will talk to the governor about my problems," Don Carlos thought. "Perhaps the governor will give me back my land. Then my family will be great again."

"I'll be very happy if you marry my daughter," he said.

Don Carlos's wife, Doña Catalina, came to the veranda. She heard the news. She was happy and excited too.

"It will be easy for you to win Lolita's love, señor," she said.

"Oh," said Don Diego. "Must I win her love? I'm sorry, but I'm not interested in that kind of thing. I don't know how to say sweet things to a woman. Must I hold her hand, and play a guitar under her window?"

He thought for a moment.

"I will send one of my servants to play a guitar for me," he said. "Please make the wedding plans. Tell me when everything is ready."

Doña Catalina and Don Carlos looked at each other in astonishment.

"This is a very strange young man," Doña Catalina thought. "Most young men enjoy winning a girl's love. And young girls want their husbands to win them. What will Lolita say about this?"

Suddenly, Lolita herself came to the veranda. She was a very beautiful young woman, with long black hair and lovely dark eyes.

"*Señorita*," said Don Diego, "I want to marry you. I've asked your father about this and he has agreed. Your parents are going to make all the plans for our wedding. A servant will tell me when everything is ready."

Lolita's black eyes flashed with anger.

"And a servant will come and play a guitar under my window!" she said. "I heard everything, señor. You're a rich man and you're from a great family. But you don't know how to win a woman's love. I'm sorry, señor, but I don't want to marry you. Goodbye."

Then she turned and walked proudly into the house.

"I don't understand," said Don Diego. "Why is she angry with me?"

"Don't worry, señor," replied Don Carlos. "My daughter will marry you. Visit her again in a few days."

When Don Diego had gone, Don Carlos talked to Lolita.

"My daughter," he said. "If you marry Don Diego, the Pulido family will be great again. Please think about this."

Lolita was sad. She wanted to help her father. But she also wanted a brave, strong husband. She wanted a man who could win her love.

———

That afternoon, Lolita was in the garden of the hacienda. The weather was very hot. The young woman sat down by a small fountain. The sound of the moving water was soft and peaceful. Soon, Lolita felt tired and she closed her eyes.

Suddenly she opened her eyes again. Somebody had touched her hand. A tall man in a long cloak was standing in front of her. He was wearing a black mask. His eyes were shining through two holes in the mask. He took off his sombrero.

Lolita knew who this man was. She had heard many stories about this thief.

"Don't be afraid," said the masked man. "I'm Señor Zorro. Perhaps you've heard of me? I'm not going to hurt you. I know about your father's problems with the governor and I'm very sorry for your family."

"Thank you," said Lolita. "But why are you here?"

"I was passing your hacienda," said Zorro. "It's a hot afternoon and I wanted to rest. I saw you and I wanted to speak to you. You're very beautiful."

"Thank you, señor," said Lolita. "But you must leave this place immediately. There's danger for you here. Somebody will see you and send for the soldiers."

"Yes," said Zorro. "You are right. I will go."

He held Lolita's hand and kissed it gently.

The young woman looked into his bright eyes and her heart began to beat faster. Quickly, she pulled her hand away from him and she ran into the house.

Zorro put on his sombrero and walked slowly from the garden. Lolita watched him from a window.

"How brave he is," she thought. "How brave—and how different from Don Diego!"

4

Lolita's Three Admirers

That evening, while the Pulido family were eating dinner, a tall stranger entered their dining room. He was wearing a sombrero, a mask and a long cloak. Don Carlos and Doña Catalina stared at him in surprise and fear.

"I'm Señor Zorro," the man said to Don Carlos. "Please don't be afraid. I'm not going to hurt you. I only want some food and drink."

Don Carlos thought quickly. He had an idea.

"Very well," he said. "But my wife is frightened. Please let me take her into another room."

"Yes, of course," said Zorro. "But the señorita must stay here with me."

Don Carlos took Doña Catalina out of the room. Zorro spoke quietly to Lolita.

"I had to return," he whispered. "I wanted to see your lovely face and I wanted to hear your soft voice again. My heart is full of love for you."

Then Don Carlos came back into the dining room. He was carrying some plates of food.

"Please sit down and eat, señor," Don Carlos said in a kind voice. "Tell us about your adventures. We've heard many stories about you."

Zorro started to talk. Don Carlos listened to him. But he was also listening for another sound—the sound of soldiers.

When Don Carlos had taken his wife into another room, he had spoken to a servant. He had told the man to ride quickly to the town and bring some soldiers from the *presidio*. Now Don Carlos wanted to keep Zorro in his house until the soldiers arrived.

"Let me bring you some wine, señor," he said. He hurried from the room.

Quietly, Lolita spoke to the masked man.

"Señor, you must go. I'm afraid. Perhaps my father has sent for the soldiers."

"He *has* sent for them—I know that," said Zorro. "But I don't want to leave you."

Don Carlos returned with some glasses and a bottle of wine. Then a servant rushed into the room.

"Señor!" he cried. "There are soldiers all around the house!"

There was a large candleholder in the middle of the table. Zorro picked it up and threw it onto the floor. The candles went out, and suddenly the room was dark. Lolita felt somebody touch her hand.

"Goodbye, señorita!" Zorro whispered in her ear. Then he went quietly out of the room. A few seconds later, Lolita heard a horse galloping away from the hacienda.

The next moment, Sergeant Gonzales and his soldiers ran into the room. They were carrying lanterns.

"Where is Zorro?" shouted Gonzales angrily.

"He has escaped," replied Don Carlos. "He rode away on his horse."

Gonzales and the soldiers rushed out of the house. They jumped onto their horses and rode after Zorro.

Don Carlos went to the veranda for a minute. Everything was quiet outside. Then suddenly, he heard the sound of a galloping horse. He felt afraid.

"Zorro is coming back," he thought. "He'll kill me because I sent for the soldiers."

But it was not Zorro's horse. Captain Ramón, the comandante of the soldiers had arrived at the hacienda.

Captain Ramón was twenty-six years old, and he was tall and handsome. A few weeks before, he had come to Los Angeles from Santa Barbara, another town in southern California.

The captain came into the dining room and he saw Lolita with her father.

"What a lovely girl!" he thought.

"I'm sorry to enter your house at this hour," he said to Don Carlos. "But we have to catch this thief, Zorro. He has done terrible things. He killed many men and women in Santa Barbara."

The captain stopped speaking. He had heard a noise. It had come from a large cupboard in the corner of the room. Suddenly, the door of the cupboard opened and a man stepped out of it. It was Zorro!

"That is a lie, señor!" he said. "I didn't kill anybody in Santa Barbara."

"What are you doing here?" asked Don Carlos in astonishment. "We heard your horse galloping away."

Zorro laughed. "My horse is very clever," he replied. "I've taught him to run away quickly. He makes a lot of noise. Then the soldiers follow him, not me. They won't catch him. He'll come back for me later."

Zorro turned to Captain Ramón.

"Now, señor," he said. "I'm going to fight you!"

Captain Ramón was very angry. He pulled his sword from its scabbard and began to fight Zorro. The captain was a good fighter, but Zorro was better. He wounded Captain Ramón in the shoulder. Blood ran from the wound.

"That's enough," said Zorro. "Good night, my friends. Don't tell lies about me again, Captain!" Then he ran out of the house. His horse was waiting at the door. Zorro jumped onto the horse and rode away into the night.

———

Captain Ramón was not badly hurt. Don Carlos's servants cleaned the blood from his shoulder. Soon, he was drinking wine and talking to Don Carlos. The captain often looked at Lolita.

Suddenly, everybody heard footsteps on the veranda. A moment later, Don Diego Vega came into the room. Everybody looked at him in surprise.

"I saw the soldiers riding from the town," Don Diego said to Don Carlos. "They told me about Zorro's visit. I was worried about you and your family."

"Thank you for coming," replied Don Carlos. "We are safe, but Zorro has escaped. He fought with Captain Ramón and wounded him in the shoulder."

The captain was looking at Lolita. Don Diego saw him looking at her and he did not like it.

"I understand," he said. "Please can I have some wine? I'm very tired. I've ridden here twice today from Los Angeles."

"But it's only four miles from here to the town," said Captain Ramón. "That's nothing for a soldier."

"But I'm not a soldier, Captain," replied Don Diego. "I'm a *caballero*—a gentleman."

Now the captain was very angry.

"What do you mean?" he said. "Can't a soldier be a gentleman too?"

Don Carlos was afraid. He did not want Don Diego and Captain Ramón to start fighting in his house.

"Please, *señores*, have some wine!" he said loudly.

Don Diego sat down beside Lolita.

"Is this captain going to stay here long?" he asked.

Lolita smiled. Don Diego was jealous of Captain Ramón!

"Your daughter is very beautiful," the captain said to Don Carlos. "May I try to win her love?"

Don Carlos thought quickly. Captain Ramón was not as rich as Don Diego. But he was a fine soldier. And he was a friend of the governor. He could help the Pulido family too.

"Well Captain, Don Diego also wants to marry my daughter," Don Carlos said. "But she hasn't said yes to him yet. So you can try to win her love too."

"Thank you," said Captain Ramón.

The captain smiled. He would win this fight. No woman wanted a weak man like Don Diego!

After Don Diego and Captain Ramón left to go back to the town, Don Carlos spoke to his daughter.

"Lolita, you have two admirers. Don Diego wants to marry you. Now the captain wants to win your love too," he said. "Who will you choose?"

"I don't like the captain," replied Lolita. "He stares at me."

"I don't understand you," said Don Carlos. "You're not interested in Don Diego, the richest young man in the country. And now you don't like this fine young officer!"

———

Lolita could not sleep that night. She thought about her third admirer. She thought about Zorro. She thought about his words, and about the touch of his hand.

"Oh, why is he a thief?" she asked herself. "I love him!"

5

A Visit From Captain Ramón

Very early the next morning, Sergeant Gonzales and his soldiers were in the town square in Los Angeles. They were getting ready for a long journey.

The door of Don Diego's house opened and Don Diego himself came out.

"Why have you left your bed so early, my friend?" asked Sergeant Gonzales.

"I couldn't sleep," replied Don Diego. "Your soldiers were making a lot of noise. What's happening?"

"We're going to ride after that thief, Zorro," said Gonzales. "He escaped from us last night."

"Did he?" said Don Diego, looking worried. "I have to ride to my hacienda today. I don't want to meet Zorro on the road."

"Don't worry, señor," said Gonzales. "Somebody saw

him on the road to Pala. That's in the opposite direction to your hacienda."

"So you're going to look for him on the Pala road," said Don Diego. "Well, good luck! Perhaps you'll catch him today!"

———

Later that morning, Don Diego started to ride towards his hacienda. But before he left Los Angeles, he sent a letter to Don Carlos Pulido.

> *Dear Don Carlos,*
>
> *I will be away from Los Angeles for two or three days. I have some business at my hacienda.*
>
> *I'm very worried about this man, Zorro. Perhaps he will come to your house again. He is very dangerous.*
>
> *Please take your family to my town house. Stay there for a few days. You will be safe there. My servants will take good care of you.*
>
> *Don Diego Vega*

When Don Carlos read this letter, he was very pleased.

"It will be good for us to stay in Don Diego's house," he said to his wife and daughter. "People will say, 'The Pulidos are guests of the great Vega family.' We will go to the town today."

Early that afternoon, the Pulido family traveled to Don Diego's house in Los Angeles. Servants brought them food and drink. Then Doña Catalina and Lolita walked through all the rooms of the fine house. They were astonished by all the rich and beautiful things that they saw there.

Later in the afternoon, Don Carlos went to the inn.

He met some important people of the town there. He told them about Don Diego's invitation to his family. After that, everybody wanted to be friends with Don Carlos. One man invited Don Carlos and Doña Catalina to his home that evening.

"We will talk and we will listen to music, señor," the man said.

Don Carlos went back to Don Diego's house. When he told his wife about the invitation, she was worried.

"But what will Lolita do this evening?" she asked.

"She must stay here," replied Don Carlos. "She'll be safe here. The servants will take care of her."

After her parents had left the house, Lolita went to the library. There were many fine books there. She opened a book and stared in astonishment at the words on the pages.

"This is a book of love poems," she thought. "But Don Diego isn't interested in love. Why does he have this book in his house?"

Suddenly, somebody knocked loudly at the front door. Lolita heard a servant open the door. Then she heard a man's voice—the voice of Captain Ramón.

"I want to talk to Señorita Lolita Pulido," the captain said.

"I'm sorry, señor, but you can't talk to her," replied the servant. "The señorita's parents have gone out this evening and she is alone."

"That's good!" said Captain Ramón.

A moment later, the captain entered the library. Lolita jumped up from her chair. She was surprised and afraid. Why did the soldier want to speak to her?

"Good evening, señorita," Captain Ramón said. "I have something to say to you. I want to marry you. Don

Diego wants to marry you too. But Don Diego is not the right man for you. He is a weak man. Everybody laughs at him. You must have a fine soldier like me as your husband! Can I win your love?"

Lolita's black eyes flashed with anger.

"Don't say bad things about Don Diego," she said. "He's my father's friend. Now, please leave this house, Captain Ramón. You are alone here with me and it isn't right. What will people think about me?"

Captain Ramón laughed.

"I'm not going to leave," he said. "I'm waiting for your answer. But first—kiss me!"

Ramón pulled Lolita towards him. She hit him across the face. But he held her tightly.

"You'll be sorry for that, my darling!" he said.

Lolita screamed, but she could not move. Captain Ramón laughed again and he bent his head towards hers. His mouth was near her lips.

Suddenly, from a corner of the room, a deep voice spoke. "One moment, señor!"

Captain Ramón looked up in astonishment. Señor Zorro was walking towards him.

"What are you doing here?" the captain whispered.

"I heard a lady scream and I came to help her," said Zorro. "You are attacking this lovely girl. You are not a caballero, señor—you are not a gentleman. Get down on the floor and apologize to the señorita. Then leave this house and don't come here again."

Captain Ramón had no sword. He could not fight Zorro. He had to do what Zorro told him. Zorro followed him to the front door and watched him walk away.

When Zorro returned to the library, Lolita ran towards him.

"Thank you, señor—oh, thank you!" she said. "That terrible man wanted a kiss from me. But now I offer that kiss to you—I offer it freely."

Zorro kissed Lolita gently on the lips.

"Señorita," he said. "My heart is full of love for you."

"And mine is full of love for you," whispered Lolita. "But you must go now. Go quickly, before my parents return."

Zorro kissed her again.

"I love you," said Lolita.

They looked into each other's eyes. Zorro pulled his cloak around him. Then he jumped through a window and disappeared into the night.

———

Later that evening, Captain Ramón was sitting in his office at the presidio—the building where the soldiers lived. He was very angry with Lolita. He wanted to punish her and her family. What could he do?

He thought for a long time. Then he had an idea. He took a pen and paper and he wrote a letter. When he had finished, he wrote out a copy of the letter. He called one of his soldiers and gave the first letter to him.

"Take this to San Francisco. Give it to the Governor of California immediately," he said.

The man left the room. Captain Ramón read the copy of the letter and he smiled.

> To the Governor of California
> Your Excellency,
> I am sorry to give you bad news. We have not captured Zorro yet. A family in Los Angeles is helping him. This makes my job very difficult. This family is the Pulido family—Don Carlos Pulido and his wife and daughter.
> Zorro ate and drank at their hacienda last night. I tried to capture him there, but he wounded me in the shoulder and he ran away. The Pulidos did not help me, they helped Zorro.
> Captain Ramón (Comandante)
> The Presidio, Los Angeles

6

The Chase

When Zorro left Lolita, he decided to ride to the presidio. He left his horse outside the building and he looked through the window of Captain Ramón's office. Captain Ramón was inside the room, sitting by a fire. There were lighted candles on a table behind him. The captain was reading a letter and he was smiling.

"What news is in that letter?" Zorro asked himself.

He entered the building quietly. Nobody saw him. He opened the door to the captain's office. Ramón looked up in surprise.

"Give me that letter, señor!" said Zorro.

When Zorro read the letter, he was very angry.

"You want to make trouble for the señorita," he said. "So you tell lies about her family to the governor."

Zorro threw the letter onto the fire. It was a copy of the letter which Ramón's messenger was taking to San Francisco. But Zorro did not know about the other copy.

At that moment, the two men heard the sound of horses. Sergeant Gonzales was returning with his soldiers.

"Gonzales!" shouted Captain Ramón. "Come quickly! Save me! Zorro is here!"

Gonzales and his men rushed into the room. Zorro pushed the candles off the table. Now the room was dark except for the light from the fire. Zorro walked to the door. The soldiers were running around the room. Sometimes they hit each other in the darkness.

Zorro ran out of the presidio and jumped onto his horse.

Gonzales and his men followed Zorro out of the building. They saw him riding away and they shot at him with their pistols. But Zorro laughed and rode faster.

"Go after him!" shouted Gonzales.

The soldiers jumped onto their horses and they rode after Zorro.

The moon was shining brightly. The soldiers could see Zorro clearly in front of them. He was riding very fast. They all rode on—Zorro in front, and the line of soldiers behind him.

They rode for a long time. Zorro's horse was getting tired. As the masked man rode, he thought of a plan.

Not far away, on the top of a small hill, there was a farm. It belonged to the Franciscan brothers of the Mission of San Gabriel. These priests did not have fine clothes or expensive things. They worked hard and they lived simply and quietly. The person who looked after the farm was an old man called Fray Felipe—Brother Felipe.

"I will visit Fray Felipe," Zorro thought.

But Sergeant Gonzales knew about the farm too.

"Zorro will stop at the brothers' house," he said to himself. "He is a friend of the Franciscans in the missions, and he often helps these priests. He'll ask Fray Felipe to hide him."

When the soldiers were near the farm, they stopped their horses and they listened. Everything was quiet. There were no lights burning in the house.

Gonzales rode up to the door of the farm and he knocked on it loudly. After a minute, Fray Felipe opened the door. He was holding a candle.

"We're chasing Señor Zorro," said Gonzales rudely. "Have you seen him tonight?"

"No," replied Fray Felipe. "I don't know this man."

"I don't believe you," said Sergeant Gonzales. "You are hiding him here, and I will find him."

"Search the house!" the sergeant shouted to his men. He got down from his horse and pushed Fray Felipe against the wall. The soldiers followed the sergeant into the house and they began to search the rooms. Gonzales went into the living room.

A man got up from a chair at the end of the room. Gonzales stared at him in astonishment.

"Don Diego!" he said. "Why are you here?"

"Don Diego!" he said. *"Why are you here?"*

"I'm returning from my hacienda," replied Don Diego. "I came to Fray Felipe's house for the night. He's a friend of my family. But why are you here, Sergeant?"

"We're chasing Zorro," replied Gonzales. "Have you seen him?"

"No," said Don Diego. "He isn't here."

"Oh," said Gonzales. "So Zorro has escaped again!"

"You look very tired, my friend," said Don Diego. "Please sit down. Fray Felipe will bring wine for you and your men."

Fray Felipe brought his best wine and the soldiers drank it. Gonzales talked with Don Diego.

"That wine was excellent," Gonzales said at last. "But now we must continue our journey."

"Where are you going next?" asked Don Diego.

"Zorro isn't here," said Sergeant Gonzales. "Perhaps he has ridden back to the town. So we must follow him."

"Can't you forget about this man, Zorro?" said Don Diego in a tired voice. "I hate fighting and violence! A quiet, peaceful life is best!"

7

At the Presidio

When Lolita's parents returned to Don Diego's house, she told them about Captain Ramón's visit.

"Señor Zorro saved me from the captain," she said. But she did not tell them about her love for Zorro.

Lolita's father, Don Carlos, was very angry. He wanted to fight Captain Ramón. But Doña Catalina stopped him.

The next day, Don Diego came back to his house in

Los Angeles. Lolita talked to him about Captain Ramón.

"Captain Ramón came here to your house and he insulted me," she said. "He behaved very badly. What are you going to do?"

"I'll talk to the governor about him," said Don Diego. He spoke in a bored voice.

"Is that all you are going to do?" said Lolita. "Won't you go to the presidio? Aren't you going to fight the captain?"

"I don't like violence," said Don Diego. "Perhaps I will talk to Captain Ramón. Now—have you thought about our wedding?"

Lolita was very angry. Why was Don Diego so weak? She thought about Zorro. How different he was! How brave and strong he was! Zorro was not afraid of Captain Ramón.

"I'm sorry, Don Diego," she said, "but I can't marry you. There is no love for you in my heart. Please don't talk to me again about marriage."

She ran out of the room. Don Diego was very surprised. Why did Lolita not want to marry him? He went to her father.

"Don Carlos," he said, "your daughter doesn't want to marry me. I'll go the presidio and I'll speak to Captain Ramón. Perhaps that will please Señorita Lolita."

———

Don Diego walked slowly towards the presidio. Captain Ramón saw him coming and stared in surprise. Don Diego had no sword with him.

"Come into my office, Don Diego," he said coldly. "Please sit down."

Don Diego sat down.

"You went to my house, Captain," he said politely.

"You insulted a young lady there. I have asked that young lady to be my wife. Perhaps you did not know about that."

Captain Ramón thought quickly. How could he make Don Diego hate Lolita? He had an idea.

"I did go to your house," he said. "But I didn't want to see Señorita Pulido. I wanted news of Señor Zorro. I must tell you something about the Pulido family. They are friends of this man, Zorro. They help him a lot. Think very carefully before you marry the daughter of that family!"

"Is this true?" asked Don Diego in surprise. "I didn't know that. This is terrible news. Thank you very much for telling me about the Pulidos, Captain."

Don Diego stood up and moved towards the door. Then he stopped.

"But what about the insult to the señorita, Captain?"

"I apologize to you, caballero," replied the captain, smiling. "I'm very sorry about it."

"Well, please don't do such a thing again," replied Don Diego. "My servant was very frightened."

When Don Diego had gone, Captain Ramón laughed for a long time. How could a man be so weak and stupid?

———

The next day, the Pulido family went back to their hacienda. Don Diego promised to visit them there. Later, he went to the inn. The fat landlord hurried to bring him some wine. Don Diego sat by the window and drank the wine slowly.

Suddenly, he saw two horsemen riding slowly along the street. A third man was with them. This man was walking between them and he was tied to their horses with ropes.

"What is happening there?" Don Diego asked the

landlord. He pointed through the window.

"They're bringing a prisoner to the judge," replied the landlord. "The prisoner is a brother from one of the missions. This priest cheated a man. He tricked him and took his money."

Don Diego looked at the prisoner. It was his friend, Fray Felipe. Don Diego was very surprised. He hurried outside.

———

Fray Felipe was taken to the town's courtroom. The judge was sitting in the courtroom. A large crowd of people was there too. Don Diego spoke to the judge.

"Why is this man here?" he asked the judge. "He's Fray Felipe. He's a good man."

"He's a thief," said the judge. "Please go home now, Don Diego."

An ugly little man stepped forward.

"I'm a hide dealer," he said. "I buy and sell animal skins. I bought ten hides from this brother. But they were not good hides. I want my money back, but the brother will not give it to me."

"The hides were very good hides," said Fray Felipe. "But this man didn't give them back to me. So I couldn't give him back his money."

"The hides smelled bad, so I burned them," said the dealer. "And now I want my money back."

"Have you anything to say, brother?" asked the judge.

"I'm telling the truth," said Fray Felipe. "The hides were good."

"You're a thief," said the judge. "You cheated this man. You took his money. You will receive a whipping in the town square. You will be hit fifteen times with a whip across your back!"

"I want my money back, but the brother will not give it to me."

8

The Whipping Post

Some soldiers took Fray Felipe from the courtroom into the town square. There was a large post in the middle of the square—the whipping post. The soldiers took off Fray Felipe's shirt and tied him to the post.

The square was full of people. They wanted to watch the whipping. Don Diego's face became pale with anger. But he could do nothing to help his friend.

One of the soldiers was holding a whip. He began to whip Fray Felipe. He hit the old brother fifteen times. Blood ran from the wounds in the priest's back, but he did not cry out. When the soldier had finished, the people laughed at the old brother. The judge laughed too.

"Give the money back to the dealer before two days have passed," the judge said to Fray Felipe. "If you don't, we'll whip you again!"

The soldiers untied Fray Felipe. He could not stand up. He was weak and he fell to the ground. Two of his friends came forward and helped him to get up. They put him in a small cart and they all began the journey back to his farm.

Don Diego went to his town house. He felt very sad and angry.

"That judge is a very bad man," he thought. "Fray Felipe did not cheat the dealer. The dealer cheated Fray Felipe. The judge was wrong to punish him. The judge and the dealer want to share Fray Felipe's money."

Don Diego called a servant.

"I don't want to stay in the town tonight," he said. "I'm going to visit my father at his hacienda."

The servant brought food and drink for the journey. Then Don Diego started to ride towards the home of his father, Don Alejandro Vega.

———

The hide dealer was in the inn, drinking wine with the judge. They laughed loudly when they talked about Fray Felipe. The dealer was happy. Everybody wanted to be his friend. Everybody wanted to buy him wine.

At last, he left the inn and started to walk home. He walked a long way out of the town. Suddenly, he stopped in surprise.

A horseman was standing in front of him. The man wore a sombrero and a long black cloak. He wore a black mask over his face. And in his hand there was a pistol.

"It's Señor Zorro!" thought the dealer. He was very afraid.

"Please don't hurt me, señor," he said. "I'm a poor man and I have no money."

"I don't want your money," replied Zorro in a terrible voice. "I'm going to punish you. Today you told lies about a poor old brother. The brother didn't do anything wrong, but he was whipped fifteen times. Now I'm going to whip you."

Zorro took a whip from under his cloak. The dealer cried out in fear. He tried to run, but he could not. Zorro began to hit the dealer with his whip. Soon the ugly little man's clothes were wet with blood.

When Zorro had finished, he left the dealer on the ground. Then he rode straight to the town. It was getting dark. Zorro rode his horse up to the inn. He did not go into it.

"Landlord!" he shouted loudly. "Bring me some wine!"

"Here's a good customer," thought the fat landlord. He

came out of the inn and went up to Zorro's horse. He could not see Zorro's face in the darkness. But then he saw his pistol.

Zorro kicked the bottle of wine from the landlord's hand. "Is the judge inside?" he asked.

"Yes, señor!" replied the landlord. He was afraid.

"Bring him out here!" Zorro said.

The landlord went into the inn. Soon he came out with the judge. The judge saw Zorro's pistol pointing at him. He tried to run away, but it was too late.

"I'm going to punish you," said Zorro. "You did a very bad thing today. That poor old brother had done nothing wrong. But you punished him cruelly. Now it's your turn."

Five men had come out of the inn. Zorro called to them.

"Tie this man to the whipping post!" he said. "If you don't, I'll shoot you!"

The men tied the judge to the post. Then Zorro gave one of the men his whip.

"Take this whip," he said. "Each of you must whip the judge five times."

The men were afraid of Zorro. They began to whip the judge. The whip hit his back twenty-five times. Then Zorro told the men to untie him.

"Carry him to his house," he said. "Let all the people see him. Let them see how Zorro punishes bad judges."

Then Zorro turned towards the fat landlord.

"Go and bring me some more wine!" he said.

The landlord hurried back inside the inn. He saw a group of young caballeros at one of the tables.

"Señor Zorro is outside," the landlord said. "If you capture him, you will get a good reward."

The caballeros were very excited. They pulled their

swords from their scabbards and they rushed outside. They saw Zorro and they ran to attack him. One caballero had a gun and he fired it at Zorro.

Zorro's horse moved suddenly. It stood up on its two back legs. Then Zorro rode into the group of caballeros.

The young men ran away from the horse. There was a lot of noise. People came running from their houses.

Zorro turned his horse and he rode quickly out of the square. "Goodbye, my friends!" he shouted.

At that moment, Captain Ramón arrived from the presidio. But there were no soldiers with him. All his soldiers had gone with Sergeant Gonzales.

The young caballeros wanted to ride after Zorro and capture him. Captain Ramón told them to go.

Thirty young caballeros chased after Zorro. Outside the town, the road divided into three roads. So the caballeros divided into three groups of ten men. The first group followed the road to San Gabriel. The second group followed the road to Fray Felipe's farm. And the third group followed the road to the hacienda of Don Alejandro Vega.

9

At the Hacienda of Don Alejandro

When Don Diego arrived at his father's hacienda, Don Alejandro was in his dining room. He was finishing his evening meal.

"Ah, Diego!" he said. "It's good to see you, my son. Sit down and have some wine. Tell me, what's the news from Los Angeles?"

"The news is terrible!" replied Don Diego. "There has been violence in the town. Fray Felipe was whipped today. And that man, Zorro, has been in Los Angeles. Nobody can catch him."

"Yes, I've heard many things about Zorro," said Don Alejandro.

"There's something else," began Don Diego. "I went to the Pulido hacienda. I asked Señorita Lolita Pulido to marry me. Her father agreed. But the señorita doesn't want to marry me."

"What?!" shouted Don Alejandro. "She doesn't want to marry a young man from the great Vega family?"

"That's right," said Don Diego. "The problem is this— she wants me to say sweet words to her. She wants me to play a guitar under her window. But these things are very boring for me, Father. I can't do them."

"Listen to me, my son," said Don Alejandro. "Señorita Lolita is the best young woman in the country. You can't buy her like a horse! You're my only son. You're nearly twenty-five. You must have a wife and you must have children. Then our family name will not die. Go back to the señorita and win her love. If you don't, you won't get my money when I die. I'll leave all my money to the

Franciscan brothers."

"But, Father—" Don Diego began.

Suddenly, the two men heard the sound of horses outside the house. A few minutes later, ten young caballeros came into the room. They were carrying swords and pistols.

"What do you want?" asked Don Alejandro in surprise.

"We're chasing Señor Zorro," replied one of the caballeros. "Did you see him on the road, Don Diego?"

"No," replied Don Diego. "But please sit down and drink some wine."

Don Alejandro's servants brought wine and cake. The caballeros took off their swords and they sat down. They began to eat and drink. Soon they forgot about Zorro. Don Alejandro told his servants to put the swords in a corner of the room.

Don Diego talked with the caballeros for a long time. At last, he stood up.

"Please excuse me, everybody," he said. "I've ridden a long way today and I'm very tired. Good night."

He left the dining room. Don Alejandro sat with the caballeros. They continued to eat and drink. Soon, they were all very drunk. They began singing.

"Where is Zorro?" one of them shouted. "Why isn't he here?"

A strong voice from the doorway answered them.

"Señores, he is here!"

The caballeros stopped laughing and talking. Zorro walked slowly into the room. He was wearing his long cloak and his black mask, and he had a pistol in his hand.

The swords of the caballeros were in the corner of the room. They could not reach them.

"Listen to me, caballeros!" said Zorro. "What kind of men are you? You sit here, drinking wine and singing. But look around you! Terrible things are happening every day in this country. The governor and his friends are only interested in money. They take money from poor people!"

"You are men from the best families in the country," he went on. "Together you are very strong. Work together against the governor and stop these bad things! Do something useful with your lives!"

Zorro talked for a long time and the caballeros listened to him. He was right, they knew that. The governor and his friends did many bad things. So the caballeros decided to work with Zorro and to fight against the governor.

"Excellent!" said Zorro.

Then Don Alejandro spoke.

"I agree with you, señor," he said. "I will help you too."

When the caballeros heard this, they were very happy.

"Good," said Zorro. "Now listen! This meeting must be a secret. Tomorrow morning, you must all go back to Los Angeles. I'll send for you when I need you. So be ready at all times! Now, good night. Don't try to follow me."

Zorro left the room. The caballeros were very excited. They began to talk about their plans for the future.

A few minutes later, Don Diego came back into the dining room.

"What is all this noise?" he said in a tired voice. "I can't sleep."

"Listen, my son," said Don Alejandro. "Señor Zorro was here. He talked to the caballeros. They are going to fight together against the governor. Now you can be a brave caballero too. You must join these men. Ride to the town with them tomorrow!"

"But Father, I don't like—" began Don Diego.

"Don't argue with me," said Don Alejandro angrily. "Do what I tell you!"

10

The Pulidos Are Arrested

The Governor of California was in San Francisco. When he received Captain Ramón's letter about the Pulido family, he was very angry.

"The Pulido family is helping that thief, Zorro," he said. "They are enemies of this country, and they are my enemies too. I will go immediately to Los Angeles and I will punish them."

The governor traveled to Los Angeles and he went to the presidio. He wanted to talk to Captain Ramón.

"Have you caught Señor Zorro yet?" he asked the captain.

"No, Your Excellency," replied Captain Ramón. "But I've sent my best soldiers to find him."

"And Don Carlos Pulido is helping Zorro?"

"Yes, Your Excellency. I found Zorro at Don Carlos's hacienda. And when the Pulidos stayed in Don Diego's house in the town, Zorro followed them. The whole family is helping him—Señorita Lolita too. They hide him and give him food."

The governor thought for a minute. Then he spoke.

"The soldiers must arrest Don Carlos and his family," he said. "I'll send the Pulidos to jail."

———

Don Carlos was sitting quietly on the veranda of his hacienda. Suddenly, he heard the sound of horses. A large group of soldiers was galloping towards the house. A sergeant was leading them.

"Are you Don Carlos Pulido?" asked the sergeant.

"Yes," replied Don Carlos.

"I have orders from his Excellency, the Governor of California. I am going to arrest you."

"But what have I done wrong?" asked Don Carlos in surprise.

"You are helping the enemies of this country."

"That's not true!" said Don Carlos. "I've never helped the enemies of this country."

"You must tell that to a judge," said the sergeant. "But now I must arrest you and take you to jail."

"To jail!" said Don Carlos. "Please let me tell my wife and daughter where I'm going. They'll be worried about me."

"I'm going to arrest them and take them to jail too," said the sergeant. "Those are my orders!"

Don Carlos's face became pale. He did not care about going to jail himself. But he did not want Doña Catalina and Lolita to go there. The jail was a horrible place. It was very dirty and it was full of thieves and murderers.

He went into the house and the sergeant followed. He told his wife and daughter the bad news. Doña Catalina looked at the sergeant. Then she spoke proudly.

"The governor has taken away our money and our land," she said. "But he can never take away our good name."

Servants brought a small carriage to the front door, and the Pulidos got into it. The carriage began its journey to Los Angeles. As they got near the town, the Pulidos saw a large crowd of people. The governor had paid these people. He had told them to stand by the road. He had told them to laugh and throw dirt at the Pulidos.

But the Pulidos looked proudly in front of them and they did not speak.

At last, the carriage stopped in front of the jail. The sergeant knocked on the heavy door and an ugly jailer came out.

"Who are these people?" he asked, smiling horribly.

"Enemies of the country," replied the sergeant. He pushed the Pulidos inside the jail. The door closed behind them.

The jailer took the Pulidos to a small dark room. He left them there and he locked the door behind him.

The room was very small and dirty. The smell was terrible. The Pulidos sat down in a corner. Tears ran down the faces of Don Carlos and Doña Catalina.

But Lolita did not cry. She was thinking about Zorro. For a moment, she felt happy. She held her father's arm.

"Don't be sad, dear Father," she said. "We'll get out of here. Perhaps a friend will rescue us!"

11

At the Jail

Later that day, Don Diego Vega was riding towards the presidio. He was going to talk to the governor. He was not hurrying. Sometimes, he stopped and looked at the beautiful flowers by the side of the road. When he arrived at the presidio, he found the governor in Captain Ramón's office.

"Welcome to Los Angeles, Your Excellency," said Don Diego.

"Thank you," said the governor. "Some very bad things are happening here. Today I had to send the Pulido family to jail."

"To jail?!" said Don Diego. "Why? Did they do something terrible?"

"They helped the thief, Zorro," replied the governor.

"They are enemies of this country and I am going to punish them."

"Oh," said Don Diego. "But I've asked Señorita Lolita to marry me."

"You must think again about that," said the governor. "Don't marry her, señor! And don't talk to anyone from the Pulido family!"

"I will think about your words," said Don Diego. "Thank you, Your Excellency."

Don Diego left the presidio and he went home.

"I'm not feeling well," he told his servant. And soon, he went to bed.

———

All that day, the ten young caballeros were waiting to hear from Zorro.

"Señor Zorro will send us a message soon," they thought. "The Pulidos are in jail. We must rescue the family!"

And that evening, when it was dark, Zorro *did* send a message to the caballeros. He asked them to meet him. All the caballeros came to the meeting and they brought their friends too. There were now twenty-six young men ready to fight with Zorro. But Don Diego was not at the meeting.

"I went to his house," said one caballero, "but Don Diego's servant came to the door. Don Diego is in bed. He is ill."

Zorro told the caballeros about his plan to save the Pulidos. Then all the young men put black masks over their faces. They rode quickly to the town.

The caballeros sat on their horses outside the jail. Zorro and four others rode up to the jail door and got off their horses. There were no lights burning inside the building and everything was quiet. Zorro knocked loudly on the door with the handle of his pistol.

At last, the ugly jailer came to the door.

"What do you want?" he asked. Then he saw Zorro's pistol. It was pointing at him. The jailer was very afraid!

"Open this door wide," said Zorro. "If you don't, I'll shoot you!"

The jailer opened the door of the jail wide, and the five men went inside. Zorro took the jailer's keys. He tied the man's feet and hands with strong rope. Then he found the door of the room where the Pulidos were prisoners. He unlocked it quickly.

One of the caballeros held up a candle. By its light, Zorro saw Lolita and her parents. When he saw the dirty room, he felt very sad and angry.

Lolita looked up and she saw Zorro. She shouted happily and ran towards him.

"You are free!" said Zorro.

Don Carlos was very surprised. But before he could say anything, the caballeros took him out of the room. Lolita and Doña Catalina followed them. When they were all safely outside, Zorro spoke to the other men.

"Take Don Carlos and his wife to the hacienda of Don Alejandro Vega. The governor's soldiers will not look for them there. I'll take care of Señorita Lolita."

Suddenly he saw Sergeant Gonzales and his soldiers riding towards the jail. Gonzales had returned to Los Angeles that afternoon. He had been drinking wine at the inn when he heard the noise from the jail. Now he was here with his soldiers, ready for a fight.

Gonzales's men had pistols. They saw Zorro and the caballeros, and they began to shoot. Quickly, the caballeros rode away with Don Carlos and Doña Catalina.

Zorro pulled Lolita up onto his horse and followed them.

Sergeant Gonzales saw Lolita with Zorro. He told his soldiers to chase them.

Zorro was riding very fast. He wanted to take Lolita to a safe place. But where could he go? He made a decision. He rode to the farm of Fray Felipe. He got down off his horse and knocked loudly on the door. After a minute, Fray Felipe opened it.

"I need your help, Brother," said Zorro. "This young lady is the daughter of Don Carlos Pulido. Please, will you hide her in your house? The governor's soldiers are following us. If they capture her, they'll take her to the jail."

"Of course I'll help you, Señor Zorro," said Fray Felipe.

Lolita got off the horse and Zorro kissed her gently on the lips. Then he jumped onto the horse and rode away. Fray Felipe took Lolita into his house and he closed the door.

Sergeant Gonzales had seen Zorro riding up to the brothers' farm. There had been two people on Zorro's horse—Zorro and the young woman. But when Gonzales saw Zorro riding away, the masked man was alone on the horse.

"So, Zorro has left Lolita Pulido with Fray Felipe," thought Gonzales.

The sergeant rode up to the house and he knocked on the door loudly with the handle of his sword. After a minute, Fray Felipe opened the door.

"Why are you making all this noise?" the old brother asked. "What do you want? We're trying to sleep."

"You are hiding the Pulido girl here!" said Gonzales rudely. He called his soldiers. "Search the house!" he told them.

The soldiers jumped down from their horses and

rushed into the house. They began to search all the rooms. Gonzales pushed Fray Felipe out of his way and he went into the living room. In the corner of the room there was a pile of animal hides. Gonzales saw something moving behind the pile. He began to walk towards it.

But before he could reach it, a young woman stood up. It was Lolita. She was holding a long sharp knife in her hand. Gonzales stopped and he stared at her in surprise. What was she going to do?

"If you come closer, I'll kill myself!" Lolita said. "That is the truth! I'm not afraid to die!"

Gonzales did not move. He did not want Lolita to kill herself. "If that happens, the governor will be very angry," he thought.

Lolita moved quickly towards the door and she ran out of the house. The soldiers' horses were outside. Lolita was an excellent rider. She jumped onto one of the horses and rode quickly away from the farm.

A moment later, Gonzales ran out of the house, shouting for his men. They got onto their horses and they began to chase Lolita. But the moon was hidden by the clouds. They could not see Lolita in the darkness.

12

The Mark of Zorro

After Zorro left Lolita at Fray Felipe's farm, he rode back to the town. He wanted to surprise somebody!

He rode to the presidio. Then he got off his horse and walked quietly to the window of Captain Ramón's office. He could see the captain inside the room. Ramón was alone. All of his soldiers were chasing the caballeros.

Zorro went inside the building and he pushed open the door to the office. The captain looked up and he saw the masked man. Zorro was pointing a pistol at him.

"Don't move! Don't make a sound!" said Zorro. "Where's the governor?"

"He's at the house of a friend—Don Juan Estado," Ramón replied.

"That's good!" said Zorro. "Come with me, Captain. We're going to visit the governor."

Zorro tied Captain Ramón's hands with rope. He pushed him out of the building.

"Get up onto my horse," said Zorro. "But don't try to trick me. If you do, I'll shoot you!"

The captain could feel Zorro's pistol against his back. He got up onto the horse and Zorro got up behind him. They rode to Don Juan's house.

Zorro knew the house well. He entered through a servant's room, pushing Captain Ramón in front of him. It was very late, but lamplight was coming from under one of the doors. Zorro opened this door. Inside the room, the governor was talking to Don Juan. The two men looked up and they stared at Zorro and Captain Ramón in astonishment.

"Señor Zorro!" said the governor. "What are you doing here?"

"You did a very bad thing today, Your Excellency," said Zorro. "You sent the Pulido family to jail. But they haven't done anything wrong."

"They're enemies of this country," said the governor. "They help thieves and murderers. They help people like you."

"Who told you these things?" Zorro replied.

"Captain Ramón told me."

"Then Captain Ramón has told you lies," said Zorro. "The Pulidos have never helped me. When I went to their hacienda, Don Carlos sent a servant for the soldiers. But when the Pulidos were staying in Don Diego's house, Captain Ramón went there and found Señorita Lolita alone. He insulted that lovely young woman and he tried to attack her. I was passing the house and heard her scream. So I helped her. That's the truth."

"Well, Ramón," said the governor. "What do you say?"

"Tell the truth, Captain," said Zorro, pointing his pistol at Ramón's face.

"Yes," said Captain Ramón quietly, after a moment. "Zorro is speaking the truth."

The governor was angry. "You are no longer an officer in my army!" he shouted.

"Then untie my hands!" Ramón said angrily. "Let me fight this thief!"

"For those words, you will die!" replied Zorro. He held the pistol in his left hand and pulled his sword from its scabbard. He cut the rope from the captain's hands. Ramón pulled his own sword from its scabbard and he rushed at Zorro. The governor and Don Juan watched from a corner of the room. Zorro was pointing his pistol at them. They could not help the captain.

"Kill him, Ramón!" shouted the governor. "If you do, I'll make you an officer again!"

Zorro and Captain Ramón fought fiercely. Each man wanted to kill the other. Suddenly, Zorro moved his sword quickly three times. He had cut a letter Z on Ramón's face—a red and bloody letter Z.

"The Mark of Zorro!" said the masked man. "You'll wear it forever, Captain! You'll wear it in your grave!"

Then he pushed his sword through Captain Ramón's body. The captain fell to the floor. He was dead.

"My work here is finished," said Zorro. "Goodbye, Your Excellency!" Then he ran out of the building and jumped onto his horse.

Zorro rode towards the town. But he rode into danger. Night was almost gone. The sun was beginning to rise in the sky. There were many soldiers on the road. They were returning to the presidio. They could see Zorro clearly in the morning light.

Sergeant Gonzales was leading his soldiers. The big man gave a great shout.

"Zorro! There he is! Capture him, men!"

The soldiers rushed at Zorro from three sides. He

*He had cut a letter Z on Ramón's face—a red and bloody
letter Z.*

turned his horse quickly, but then he had to stop. Another rider was coming towards him very fast. Zorro stared in astonishment. The rider was Lolita! Six or seven soldiers were chasing her.

"Señor!" she shouted. "Help me! I can't ride much further. My horse is very tired."

Zorro turned his horse again. He and Lolita rode towards Los Angeles. The soldiers chased them. Zorro and Lolita galloped into the town and crossed the town square.

Suddenly Lolita's horse fell. Zorro caught her in his arms.

"Quickly!" said Zorro. "We must go to the inn!"

He jumped from his horse and he pulled Lolita with him. They ran to the inn and Zorro pushed the door open. The fat landlord was very frightened. He ran out onto the square. Zorro shut the door and all the windows.

"There are enemies all around us," he said to Lolita. "Perhaps this is the end for us."

"I've given you my love," replied Lolita. "I won't leave you now. We will live together—or we will die together!"

13

"Take Off Your Mask, Señor!"

Zorro looked out of a window. The square was full of soldiers. He saw Don Juan Estado, Don Alejandro Vega and the governor too.

"Señor," said Lolita. "Please make me a promise. If we are going to die, please take off your mask. Please show me who you are."

"Yes, my love," replied Zorro. "If we can't escape, I will show you my face. I make you that promise!"

They heard a loud noise from outside. The soldiers were starting to attack the door of the inn. Zorro pointed his pistol at the door and fired the gun. Immediately, the soldiers started to shoot at the door from the other side. But the door was strong and it did not break.

Then, everything was quiet for a moment. Zorro and Lolita heard the voice of Sergeant Gonzales.

"Open the door, Señor Zorro!" he shouted. "If you open it now, we won't kill you!"

"I don't believe you, Sergeant!" shouted Zorro. He laughed.

The soldiers began to attack the door again. This time, the door began to break.

Zorro and Lolita stood in the middle of the room. Zorro held his sword in his hand, ready to fight.

"It's nearly the end, my love," he said to Lolita.

"Hold me in your arms and kiss me," said Lolita. "Then show me your dear face."

Zorro kissed her and began to untie his mask.

But suddenly, they heard a new noise from the square—a different noise. The soldiers stopped attacking the door.

Zorro rushed to the window. He saw twenty-six fine young horsemen riding into the square, with their swords in their hands.

"My brave caballeros!" he said. "They will help us now."

The caballeros stopped their horses in front of the governor.

"We want to speak with you," their leader said. "Many bad things are happening in this country. These things are wrong and we want to change them. You cheat the brothers in the missions. And often, poor and helpless men are beaten. Then yesterday, the noble Pulido family were sent to jail. We have rescued them. But these things must stop!"

"Well, what do you want me to do?" asked the governor nervously.

"First—the Pulido family must never be sent to jail again," said the leader. "Second—you must let Señor Zorro go free. He hasn't done anything wrong. He has only stolen from thieves. He has only whipped people who hurt the poor and the weak."

"No!" cried the governor. "I won't let Zorro go free."

"Señor, we are the sons of the best families in this country," the young caballero replied. "We're very strong. If your soldiers attack us, we'll fight against you. If you hurt Señor Zorro, you'll lose the job of governor."

The governor looked at Don Alejandro Vega.

"Don Alejandro," he said, "you know these young men. Please help me."

"No," replied Don Alejandro. "These young caballeros are right. I agree with them and I agree with Señor Zorro."

"But Zorro is a murderer," said the governor. "He murdered Captain Ramón."

"No," said Don Juan Estado. "The captain died in a fight between gentlemen. It was a fair fight."

"Very well," said the governor quietly. "I'll go back to San Francisco now. Zorro can go free. But Don Alejandro must promise to take care of this town."

"I promise you that," said Don Alejandro.

"That is good," said the leader of the caballeros. "Don Alejandro is a fine man." He turned towards the inn.

"Señor Zorro!" he shouted. "You are safe. Come out now!"

The door of the inn opened and Zorro came out. Lolita was holding his arm. He took off his sombrero.

"Good morning, everybody," he said.

"Take off your mask, señor!" said the governor. "I want to see your face."

Zorro laughed and took off his mask. Everybody stared in astonishment. Lolita looked up at him, happy and surprised.

"Don Diego!" she said.

Don Alejandro walked forward.

"Don Diego—my son, my son!" he said proudly.

"Yes, Father," said Don Diego. "I'm Señor Zorro."

"And which man am I going to marry?" asked Lolita. Her dark eyes looked up at him proudly. "Am I going to marry Señor Zorro or Don Diego Vega?"

"Well, which man do you love?" asked Don Diego.

"Both of them!" she said, laughing.

Points for Understanding

1

Sergeant Gonzales talks to his soldiers about Zorro. Gonzales hates the masked man. But two of his sentences show good things about Zorro. Which sentences are these?

2

Zorro wins his sword fight with Sergeant Gonzales. Gonzales is "ready to die", but then the men from the town arrive. Was Zorro going to kill the sergeant—what do you think? Give your reasons.

3

1 Señorita Lolita does not want to marry Don Diego Vega. What are her reasons?
2 Her father is unhappy about Lolita's decision. Why?

4

1 Zorro fights Captain Ramón. Why?
2 "I don't understand you," Don Carlos says to his daughter.
   (a) Why does he say this?
   (b) There is something which Don Carlos does not know. What is this?

5

"Don Diego is a weak man," Ramón says to Lolita. "Everybody laughs at him."
   Why do people laugh at Diego? Find some sentences from the first five chapters which show their reasons.

6

"Can't you forget about this man, Zorro?" Don Diego asks Sergeant Gonzales.
   Why does he say this? What does Gonzales think about Diego's reasons? What do *you* think about his reasons?

7

"When Don Diego had gone, Captain Ramón laughed for a long time."

What does the captain think about the reason for Don Diego's visit? Why does the visit make the captain laugh?

8

Zorro whips the judge and the hide dealer. Does this remind you of any sentences about Zorro from earlier in the book?

9

In this chapter, Don Alejandro becomes angry with his son twice. What are his reasons?

10

"Don't be sad, dear Father," Lolita says to Don Carlos. "Perhaps a friend will rescue us."
Who is she thinking about?

11

"I will think about your words," Don Diego tells the governor.
Is Diego telling the truth—what do you think? Give your reasons.

12

Why is this chapter called "The Mark of Zorro"?

13

Sergeant Gonzales tells Zorro, "If you open the door now, we won't kill you."
Zorro does not believe him. Why not?

Exercises

Making Sentences 1

Write questions for the answers.

1 *When does this story take place?*
....
This story takes place in about 1822.

2 *Where*
....
This story takes place in California.

3 *What*
....
The characters speak Spanish.

4 *Was*
....
No, Los Angeles was not a big city then. It was a small town.

5 *Who*
....
Zorro helped the poor and the weak.

6 *Who*
....
Zorro was Don Diego Vega.

7 *Did*
....
Yes, Don Diego had a lot of money.

8 *What*
....
Don Diego liked music, poetry and quiet conversation.

9 *Who*
....
Captain Ramón was the comandante of the soldiers in Los Angeles.

10 *Who*
....
The Pulidos were an old and noble family.

64

Grammar Focus 1: *made* + adjective

Write sentences with *made* + an adjective, using the prompts.

1 Lolita wouldn't kiss Captain Ramón. Captain Ramón was angry.
Lolita made Captain Ramón angry.

2 Lolita did not want to marry Don Diego. Don Diego was sad.

3 Zorro saved Lolita from Captain Ramón. Lolita was happy.

4 Sergeant Gonzales drank a bottle of bad wine. He was ill.

5 Captain Ramón wanted to marry Lolita. Don Diego was jealous.

Correct the Mistakes

Correct the mistake in each sentence.

1 Don Diego payed for all the drinks.
Don Diego paid for all the drinks.

2 If you open the door, we don't kill you.

3 If Zorro come here, we will fight him.

4 Don Diego never hurrys anywhere.

5 If Ramón hurts Lolita, Zorro kills him.

The Man in the Mask

Complete the gaps. Use each word in the box once.

> beaten   watching   Zorro   reward   shadows   eyes   mean
> kind   punish   cruelly   mask   body   weak   anything
> friend   towards   forward   clearly   fear   wide
> replied   ago   holes   pointed   truth

The stranger stood in the dark [1] .... _shadows_ .... by the door. His
large sombrero was pulled down over his [2] .... He wore a
long dark cloak around his [3] ....

The landlord hurried [4] .... him. Then the stranger
stepped [5] .... into the light. Now everybody could
see him [6] .... The landlord stopped and cried out in
[7] .... Gonzales's eyes were [8] .... with
surprise. The stranger was wearing a black [9] ....
There were two [10] .... in the mask. Through these
holes, his bright eyes were [11] .... everything.

'I'm Señor [12] ....,' said the man. 'And I'm here to
speak to you.' He [13] .... at Gonzales.

'What do you [14] ....?' asked Gonzales.

'I know what [15] .... of man you are, Sergeant Gonzales,'
[16] .... Zorro. 'Four days [17] ....
you stopped a man on the road and beat him [18] ....
The man was poor and [19] .... He hadn't done
[20] .... wrong. I'm a' [21] .... of that
poor man. I've come to [22] .... you!'

Zorro was telling the [23] .... Gonzales had
[24] .... a man on the road. The sergeant remembered
that. But then he remembered the governor's [25] ....
too, and he smiled.

'Very well, Señor Zorro,' he said. 'We will fight.'

Words From the Story

S	W	O	R	D	H	I	D	E	S
L	M	A	S	K	A	S	R	C	C
S	C	A	E	A	A	G	I	E	L
T	H	I	R	T	S	K	N	N	A
L	P	E	G	R	C	H	S	E	N
A	S	H	E	I	E	A	U	M	D
T	W	T	A	C	O	S	L	I	L
W	E	T	N	K	L	N	T	E	O
C	A	P	T	U	R	E	L	S	R
I	R	N	J	A	I	L	S	P	D

Find words in the square with the meanings below. The numbers in brackets show the number of letters in each word.

1 to take someone to a police station or
   military prison to await charge or trial (6) ....*ARREST*.......

2 to take prisoner (7) ....

3 opposite of friends (7) ....

4 animal skins (5) ....

5 a tavern or place to drink wine (3) ....

6 to be rude to someone (6) ....

7 prison (4) ....

8 the person who runs an inn (8)

9 a piece of cloth that hides or protects the face (4) ....

10 a soldier with three stripes on his arm (8) ....

11 a long knife for fighting (5) ....

12 an unfair or bad action done to fool someone (5) ....

67

Word Pattern: plurals of words ending in -y

Singular	Plural
enemy	enemies
story	stories
play	plays
boy	boys

Notice that the plural ending for *enemy* and *story* is different from the ending for *play* and *boy*.

When there is a vowel (*a, e, i, o* or *u*) before the final y, the plural ending is –ys.

When there is a consonant (*b, c, d, f, g, h, j, k, l, m, n, p, q, r, s, t, v, w, x, y, z*) before the final y, the plural ending is –ies.

Write the plurals of these words.

	Singular	Plural
1	bay	
2	penny	
3	diary	
4	toy	

This rule also applies to verbs used for the third person in the Present Simple (eg *she prays*).

Complete the gaps using the correct form of the verb in brackets.

1 Fray Felipe has a donkey. It ......*carries*...... (**carry**) water.

2 Don Diego always .... (**pay**) for drinks in the inn.

3 The Governor .... (**worry**) about Zorro.

4 Captain Ramón .... (**say**) Zorro is a bad man.

5 Sergeant Gonzales .... (**buy**) wine every day.

6 Don Diego never .... (**hurry**). He goes everywhere slowly.

7 The hide dealer .... (**bury**) his animal skins in the sand. He tricks Fray Felipe.

8 When Lolita .... (**marry**) Zorro, she will be happy.

9 Don Diego often .... (**stay**) with the Franciscan brothers.

10 Don Carlos .... (**deny**) helping Zorro.

Grammar Focus 2: *when/if* + future tense

Write full sentences with *when/if* + the future tense, using the prompts.

1 Lolita / marry Zorro / happy.
   When Lolita marries Zorro, she will be happy.

2 Lolita / marry Ramón / unhappy
   If

3 Ramón / catch Zorro / happy
   When

4 Sergeant Gonzales / kill Zorro / rich
   If

5 Zorro / visit Lolita / captured
   If

6 Don Carlos and his family / go to prison / frightened
   When

Making Sentences 2

Put the words in the correct order to make full sentences.

1 He pulled with his horse and Lolita jumped from him.
   He jumped from his horse and pulled Lolita with him.
   ....

2 Gonzales knocked up his horse loudly and rode to the door on it.
   ~~Ga~~
   ....

   ....

3 I am hide because I sell skins and buy a dealer.
   ....

4 Zorro jumped off into the night and rode onto his horse.
   ....

5 the love of Don Diego was interested in women not winning.
   ....

   ....

Words From the Story 2

Unjumble the letters to find words from the story, and complete the sentences.

1 **drawer**   The governor offered a big .... for the
               capture of Zorro.

2 **desarter** Don Carlos was .... and taken to jail.

3 **recaput**   The soldiers tried to kill or .... Zorro.

4 **seemine**   The governor said that the Pulidos were ....
               of Spain.

5 **estangre** Gonzales held the rank of ....

70

Writing

Complete the governor's poster.

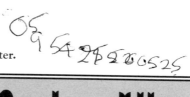

Wanted Dead or Alive
Reward 10,000 pesos

Name ....

Description ....

....

Weapons ....

....

....

Crimes ....

....

....

Macmillan Education
Between Towns Road, Oxford OX4 3PP
Macmillan Publishers Limited
Companies and representatives throughout the world

ISBN 978-0-230-02921-7
ISBN 978-1-4050-7699-9 (with CD edition)

This publication is based on *The Mark of Zorro* and characters and
elements from stories copyrighted in the name of Zorro Productions, Inc.
The Zorro name is a registered trademark of Zorro Productions, Inc.

This retold version by Anne Collins for Macmillan Readers
First published 2000
Text © Macmillan Publishers Limited 2000, 2002, 2005
Design and illustration © Macmillan Publishers Limited 2000, 2002, 2005

This edition first published 2005

Illustrated by Vladimir Pisarev
Original cover template design by Jackie Hill
Cover illustration by Michael Grimshaw

Printed in Thailand

2015   2014   2013
8   7   6   5   4

with CD pack

2015   2014   2013
16   15   14   13